for Paul Walton, with great affection, admiration, and grat...
Commissioned by Caroline to mark his 40th Birthday

Walton's Paean

Fairly fast and festive ♩ = *c.*100

Tuba

Gt. *f*

cresc.

cresc.

ff

ff

cresc.

Printed in Great Britain

OXFORD UNIVERSITY PRESS, MUSIC DEPARTMENT, GREAT CLARENDON STREET, OXFORD OX2 6DP

Clifton Village, 27 January 2018